TENNIS

CONTENTS

ABOUT THE AUTHOR

Anne Pankhurst spent ten years as Coach Education
Director for the Lawn Tennis Association, developing
courses, books and videos for coaches and clubs.
She is currently working with coaches and players in
North America and the Far East, as well as in Britain.

1 GETTING STARTED

Nothing beats the thrill of watching a top-class tennis match. You may have seen Wimbledon or the Davis Cup on television, or you may have been lucky enough to go to a big final. The tension that mounts as the players strive for victory is unbelievable. You find yourself on the edge of your seat, biting your nails, willing one of the players to score a point. The match play is fantastic to watch, and you can only marvel at the skill, athleticism, and mental toughness of the competitors.

But you don't have to confine yourself to sitting and watching. With hard work and good coaching, you can become a good tennis player – and, who knows, **you may even compete at Wimbledon one day!**

The sport's most complete player, Roger Federer, holds the Wimbledon trophy aloft.

Greg Rusedski and Tim Henman display essential skills such as co-ordination and quick reactions.

A new challenge

Many players start with Mini Tennis, which is specially designed for younger children. The ball is slower, the rackets are the right size, and you are able to cover the court with ease, so you can become a competent player in quite a short time. But now, maybe, you are ready for a new challenge. You want to find out more about the game, and you are keen to improve your skills.

To play tennis well, and to improve, you need to work at the following:

- **Co-ordination** You need to be able to do at least two things at once! For example, you need to run and hit, or separate your arms to send the racket and the ball in different directions for the serve.

- **Reactions** You need to be able to get to the right place on the court to contact the ball at the right time. The ball travels fast from your opponent's racket and you need to react and move very quickly.

- **Stroke play** You need to learn how to play a variety of shots – and be equally good at them all!
- **Technical knowledge** You need to know the technical points of the game – how to start a point off with a serve, hitting the ball after it has bounced once for the groundstrokes, and before it has bounced for the volley.

All of this is easier as you get older and if you practise. You will probably play other sports, and the bonus is that the skills you have learned in different games are essential for tennis. For example, being able to move quickly in different directions and being able to keep your balance.

Tennis is fun to play at all levels, and with the help of this book, you will soon become a player to be reckoned with. Learn how to be:

- **A good tactician** Find out where to be on the court so you have the best chance of receiving shots, and where to hit the ball to make it difficult for your opponent to return.
- **A good technician** Find out how to improve your technique so that you hit the ball into court more consistently, more accurately, and harder.
- **The fittest player** Pace and stamina are essential, and you need to be supple and athletic enough to move around the court and play shots.
- **The toughest player** You can be a skilful player, but it is just as important to have the mental toughness to out-play your opponent.

You can also find out about different sorts of competitions and tournaments in tennis, and become word perfect on the rules of the game. Work hard and practise as often as you can, but remember, above all, to have fun!

The great thing about tennis is that it is so versatile. It can be played:

- All year round.
- Indoors or outdoors.
- On different surfaces (grass, clay, hard courts).
- With two players (singles) or four players (doubles).
- At any age.
- A match can last for hours, or be over in no time!

TACTICAL WIZARDRY

There are some basic, but important, tactical rules to learn if you want to be a good player. You need to use them in the order below. But remember, your opponents are probably using them too! These tactical rules apply in every situation in every point – for the serve, in a rally, or volleying.

The golden rules

1 It sounds obvious, but the player who hits the ball once more over the net and into the court cannot lose! You must learn to be consistent and keep the ball in play. Getting the ball 'over and in' is the first rule of match play.

2 Moving the ball from one side to the other makes your opponent run – and more likely to make mistakes. So the next rule is: be accurate. It is much easier to hit the ball if you stand still – so don't give your opponent that option! Try to make the ball travel over as many lines as possible once it has bounced – your opponent has to run much further and may give you an empty court to hit the next shot into.

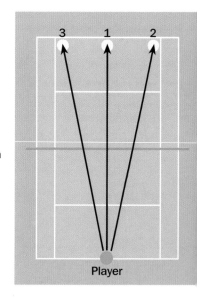

PRACTICE 1

Practise moving the ball from side to side of the court.

- Firstly, hit the ball straight in front of you, following line number **1** in the diagram and aiming to place the ball on the spot marked in yellow.

- Secondly, hit the ball following line number **2**.

- Thirdly, hit the ball down line number **3**.

- Now practise all three lines until you can aim the ball consistently and accurately.

Lleyton Hewitt keeps a close eye on the ball.

TACTICAL WIZARDRY

3 Make sure you always get back to a good position so that you are ready for the next shot. In practice diagram 2 (below) you can see that this is about halfway between your opponent's possible lines of return – it's geometry! Don't be caught out watching your last shot and not being ready for the next one.

PRACTICE 2

Try this out by practising moving into position for the return of serve.

Think about where your opponent is likely to hit the ball and move into a position that allows you to cover that area.

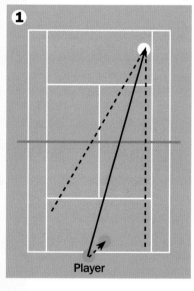

- Imagine that you are serving from the left-hand side of the court (diagram 1). The lines your opponent may follow when returning the ball are marked by a dotted line. Once you have served, move into position about half-way between each possible return.

- Try the same practice on the right-hand side of the court (diagram 2).

- Once you have practised serving and moving into position for the return, get someone to return the ball for you, so that you can improve your speed and reactions.

4 Try to hit your best shot more often so you have a good chance of winning the point. Many players find that their forehand is their best shot, but for some players – Justine Henin-Hardenne and Tim Henman, for example – their backhand is better. With others it is the serve, and with Andre Agassi it is the return of serve.

5 Finally, your opponent will always have weaknesses, or shots that he or she finds more difficult. Try to work out which these are as soon as you can, and hit the ball to that shot more often so that you get a weaker return. But don't overdo it – players improve with practice!

Justine Henin-Hardenne is famed for her powerful backhand.

TACTICAL WIZARDRY

There are some important principles to remember and practise for singles and doubles.

In singles you will always be in one of five 'game situations' when you hit the ball.

1. You will be serving or...

2. ...you will be returning the serve or...

3. ...you and your opponent could be at the back of the court, rallying and trying to outwit each other or...

4. ...you could be approaching the net to volley or...

5. ...your opponent could be approaching the net to volley.

TACTICAL WIZARDRY

In doubles, you will have a partner. The same situations apply, but doubles is about teamwork.

After the serve you need to try to stay together, either at the net or at the back of the court. If one of you is at the net and the other at the back there are big spaces for your opponents to hit the ball into.

Getting to the net gives you the best chance of winning the point.

Serena and Venus Williams using the width of the court, giving them angles to hit into.

Most young players know that sound technique is important. The basic strokes are groundstrokes (forehands and backhands), serves and volleys. All the other shots are based on these so, for example, the lob and return of serve are modified groundstrokes, drive and stop volleys are changes to volley

Amelie Mauresmo's mastery of a range of skills makes her a tough opponent.

technique, and the smash is a modified serve.

You can change the basic shot by changing the path of the racket or by adding spin. Once you have the basic shots it is easy to learn extra, and different, shots that will give you many more options in the game.

TECHNICAL SKILLS

Basic forehands and backhands

Groundstrokes are used when the ball has bounced once. This means that you are likely to be nearer the baseline than the net, so the ball will usually need to be hit up and over the net – and over a long distance. To achieve these, you need to do the following:

- Make sure you have a comfortable grip. On the forehand this would probably be a semi-western (picture 1), and on the backhand, it could be double handed (dominant hand at the bottom of the handle, picture 2) or single handed (picture 3). Whichever way you hold the backhand, make sure your bottom hand has a backhand grip.

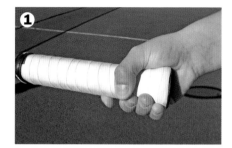

- Move towards the ball, turning your hips and shoulders and taking the racket back at the same time.
- Swing the racket from behind you to contact the ball to your side and in front. The swing should be a long one to get the ball to the back of the court.
- The racket must then follow through in front of you, and probably over your opposite shoulder. As you bend your elbow, it should point in the direction you have hit the ball.
- Move towards a good court position for the next shot.

Carlos Moya shows great control and power because he uses his knees.

As you get better, and also stronger, you will begin to use your knees more at the beginning of the action. This will help you to hit the ball harder.

Practising groundstrokes

To develop your technical skills you need to practise. Here are three ideas that may help you to improve the consistency and accuracy of your groundstrokes.

Learn to master groundstrokes and your overall game will improve rapidly.

PRACTICE 3

- To learn consistency, put a series of markers in a line about 1 metre inside the baseline (diagram 1). Practise rallying with a partner to get the ball 'over and in', between the markers and the baseline. Try to get to 50 without stopping. (You can hit shorter balls, but do not count them in the total.)

- To learn accuracy, try to hit the ball to one corner and then the other (diagram 2). Try for 50, or a personal best.

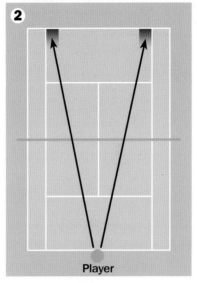

2

Player

- Take a partner and try to combine accuracy with consistency. Try hitting straight down the line with your partner returning the ball cross court (diagram 3).

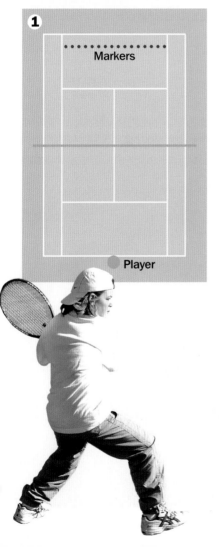

1

Markers

Player

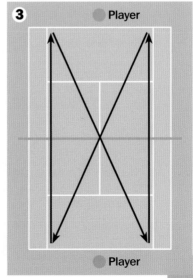

3

Player

Player

TECHNICAL SKILLS

Adding spin and slice

As you improve, you can add spin, topspin and slice to your groundstrokes.

Spin makes the ball more difficult for the opponent to 'read,' and from your point of view, it usually gives the ball a better chance of going in. In theory, if you hit it with enough spin, you can hit it as hard as you like!

Topspin

This makes the ball go higher over the net, land a bit shorter in the court, and then bounce up sharply. So you need to think about when to use it, and where your opponent is positioned.

To hit topspin you must start the racket head below the ball, and bring the strings up sharply behind the ball, turning your wrist as you do so. The follow-through must be high to lift the ball up and over the net.

Direction of ball

Racket strings

Slice

This makes the ball go in a flatter flight path, closer to the net, but it travels further. When it bounces, it moves back towards the net.

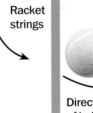

Racket strings

Direction of ball

To hit slice you must start the racket head above the ball and bring the strings down the back of the ball. The racket should then finish well in front of you, at about waist level. If you have a double-handed backhand, you need to use one hand on the backhand slice. It is also easier to hit good slice if you push your non-racket arm back as you move your racket arm forwards through the ball.

Basic serves

The serve should be an offensive weapon, but it takes time to practise and develop. For the basic serve you need to:

- Stand sideways to the line with your feet comfortably apart, for balance.
- Hold the racket and the ball in front of you and relax.
- Move your arms in different directions – one to place the ball, and the other to move the racket over a long distance so that it hits the ball hard.
- Place the ball up and in front of you, so that the racket head meets it with the arm fully extended.
- Allow for the follow-through, which is to the opposite side of the body.
- Prepare for your opponent to return the serve!

As you get older you will get stronger, and that means the serve will improve.

- You will begin to rotate the hips and shoulders, which means your knees will bend.
- This enables you to push against the ground, driving your body up towards the ball.
- As a result, you will begin to leave the ground, and then land inside the court on your front foot. When you are learning to serve, your back foot comes forwards to help you get your balance and be ready for the return.

*Greg
Rusedski
launches
one of his
formidable
first serves.*

Marat Safin
following through
on his serve.

Spin

Topspin and slice can be used on the serve, too. Most players put some spin on their second serve to help keep it in the court. They hit the first serve hard!

Direction of ball

Racket strings

The easiest spin to use is slice. To hit this, you need to use your wrist to bring the racket strings around the outside of the ball as you make contact with it. The ball then moves to the left as it leaves you (if you are right-handed), and on the bounce near the sideline it veers off to the opponent's right. If you serve slice down the centre, the ball will come into the opponent's body.

Topspin is a bit harder to learn, and more difficult to make effective. You need to place the ball slightly further back on the toss, and to your left. You then bring the strings from below the ball and up and over it. The follow-through is sometimes easier on your racket side to start with. The ball goes higher over the net and should then dip quickly into the service box, before kicking up after the bounce. If you work with a coach, you will probably be shown a number of different ways to help you learn the topspin action.

Practising your serve

The serve is one of the most important parts of your game and is worth constant practice.

PRACTICE 4

Practise improving the consistency and accuracy of your serve.

To learn consistency, practise from both sides of the court. Always keep the same position on the baseline and the same body position. Aim to get the ball in the service box as close to the service line as possible. Practise first and second serves each time.

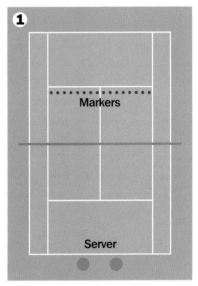

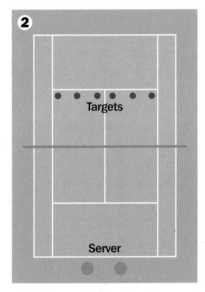

- Place some markers on the court, just inside the service line (diagram 1). Aim to get the ball between the markers and the service line. Practise first and second serves each time.

- To learn accuracy, place three targets on the court one in the sideline corner, one in the centre corner, and one in the middle of the service line (diagram 2). Practise hitting the serve to each in turn, and then get a friend to tell you where to serve it.

- Play a service game against yourself. If you get the serve in on the first point it is 15-0, if you double fault on the next point it is 15-all. Play to the end of the game. Next time get a better score.

- All of these practices can be done with spin on the second serve.

- As you improve, make sure you have a receiver at the other end – it adds pressure!

TECHNICAL SKILLS

Andre Agassi is master of the return.

Return of serve

To begin with, this is a basic forehand or backhand, but you will need to improve on this as you become more skilled. When the opponent serves a hard and fast serve, you will need to have a short and low take-back, and just bring the racket up through the ball – there won't be time for a long take-back.

You will also need to be able to hit the ball at full stretch (this can also happen in the rally), so instead of being slightly sideways as you hit the ball, you will be facing the net. The danger is that you may contact the ball too far back, and not to the side and in front of you.

The volley

When you get a short ball in a rally, you will move forwards towards the net and then volley, which means hitting the ball before it bounces on your side of the net. You need to volley well and that often depends on the approach being good.

Approaching the net

- Make sure you move forwards on a 'short' ball from your opponent.
- Hit that ball deep towards the baseline to give yourself more time to get to the net.
- As the opponent hits the return, you need to stop, split step, and then move forwards to the ball. The split step helps you check, balance, and change direction if you need to.

Short and sharp

Because the volley is hit before the bounce, and the ball is still travelling quite fast towards you, you need to have a short, sharp action.

- Make sure you have the racket head up – above your wrist – so that you can deal with a hard, fast ball.
- Keep your knees bent so that you can move into the volley – don't wait for the ball to come to you.
- If the ball is below the net, bend your knees even more so that you keep the racket up and under control.
- Your elbows should be forward so that you can keep the action

short, in front and to the side.

- Keep your wrist firm and 'locked' as you hit the ball in front of your shoulder, and then stop the follow-through as soon as you can – keep the action as short a possible.
- Aim to hit the ball down into your opponent's court.

If you have a double-handed backhand, you need to learn to hit volleys with one hand. That usually means thinking about what you do with the other hand.

Tim Henman clinches another point with a volley close to the net.

Practising your volley

PRACTICE 5

This exercise will help you to improve the consistency and accuracy of your volleys.

- Put a series of markers around the court and practise volleying the ball to the markers.

- To move in the game-real situation, get a friend to feed you the ball at different lengths. Choose the short ball, and then play an approach shot and then a volley. Make sure you win the point with a maximum of two volleys.

- As with all practice sessions, ask your coach or friends to feed you as many balls as possible to give you plenty of opportunity to improve your skills.

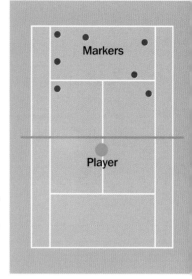

Markers

Player

Drive volley

Sometimes the short ball will be high in the air, and you can try to hit it before it bounces. This has the great advantage of getting the ball back much faster!

- Make sure you watch the ball very carefully.
- As you move forwards, turn the shoulders and take the racket back.
- Swing the racket forwards so that you contact the ball in front, and to the side of you.
- Hit the ball down into the court away from the opponent.
- Move towards the net to deal with a volley.

Watch the ball very carefully when you volley.

Tommy Haas launches a lob.

The lob

As your game improves and you play better opponents, you will find players coming to the net to volley. You need to learn the lob to send the ball over their head and to land just inside their baseline.

To lob you need to learn disguise!

- Take the racket back, as normal for a forehand or backhand.

- As you swing the racket forwards, bring the racket up under the ball and lift it high over the opponent.

  - The follow-through should be high over your shoulder.

    - If you turn your wrist at the same time you will add topspin, and this will help keep the ball in the court. Topspin, as you know, brings to ball shorter in the court.

TECHNICAL SKILLS

The smash

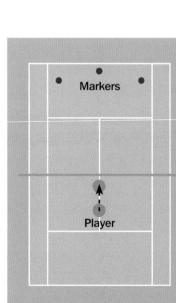

If you approach the net to volley, you will probably find that your opponent sends up a lob. The smash is the answer to a bad lob, and it enables you to take back the initiative. It is like the serve, but the opponent has put the ball in the air for you.

- First, you need to move quickly backwards – take sideways steps and never take your eye off the ball!
- Get back under the ball, and take your racket back as you move. It helps to keep your balance if you use your other arm to 'point' towards the ball.
- Try to 'serve' at the ball. Hit it at full stretch and let the follow-through happen, just as it does when you serve.
- Try to hit the ball away from your opponent – maybe deep into the corners, or even cross-court.
- Recover quickly and move forwards again to the net, ready to volley.

PRACTICE 6

Practising your smash.

This exercise will help you to learn consistency and accuracy.

- Put a series of markers in a line about 1 metre inside the baseline and practise smashing the ball so that it hits the marker.

- Each time you hit the smash, return to the net so that you are ready for your next shot.

- To practise the sequence in a game situation, start from the net each time.

4 FITNESS FANATICS

As your game develops, you will need to be much fitter in order to play well, both tactically and technically. The game is faster, could go on for longer, and the shots will be hit harder.

You should always warm up and cool down properly because that helps prevent injuries and stiffness.

You need to develop:

- **Movement** The game is faster, and it is vital to get to the next shot with good footwork.
- **Speed** – of your whole body (to reach the ball), and of your racket arm (to make sure the racket head is moving fast to hit the ball hard).
- **Stamina** You never know how long a match will last, and you need to hit all the strokes as well at the end as at the beginning.
- **Co-ordination** You need to be able to do different things with different parts of your body, and at different speeds. For example, moving your feet quickly and your arms slowly.
- **Flexibility** You must reach balls that are high above your head, those that are very low and wide – and those that come straight at you.
- **Strength** Constant movement and hitting the ball hard means that you have to be strong.

Serena Williams' fitness gives her extraordinary power on court.

FITNESS FANATICS

There are specific tennis practices to help you improve your movement, speed, stamina, co-ordination and flexibility.

Movement

PRACTICE 7

Practise moving around the court.

For both exercises, face the net at all times with your racket in your hand.

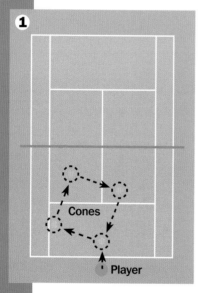

1 Cones / Player

2

- Put a number of cones on the ground (diagram 1).

- Run to the first cone quickly, and move around it with little steps.

- Run to the next one and move around that.

- Repeat until you have gone round all the cones.

- Start in the middle of the baseline (diagram 2).

- Keeping your head up, move with side steps to the sideline.

- Practise your groundstroke off an open stance.

- Push off your outside foot, cross over your feet and then sidestep to the other sideline. Then side step back to your starting position. Repeat several times.

Speed

Make sure you are warm before you start work! You need five friends to help you.

- Form a line behind the baseline ready for a relay race. The first person runs as fast as possible to the net, and back, to touch the hand of the second person, and so on. Run through the whole team twice.
- Face a partner, who throws single balls to you over the singles court for five to seven seconds, which means around five balls. You have to reach every ball, and at least touch it with your racket.
- Place five cones on the court, each with a ball on the top. Run and collect the ball off each one, and bring it back to the baseline in turn.

Stamina

PRACTICE 8

Increase your stamina.

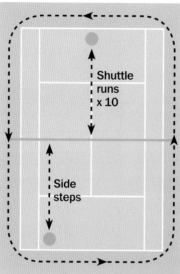

Shuttle runs x 10

Side steps

Playing other games, such as unihoc, 5-a-side football or Swedish handball, will help to improve your stamina, but the following is a stamina-improving exercise you can practise on the tennis court.

- Starting on the baseline, run to the net and back. Repeat 10 times.

- Run a complete circuit around the court.

- Go to a corner where the sideline meets the baseline. Side step to the net and back and repeat several times.

- Alternatively, you could run for 15 minutes without stopping.

Co-ordination

- Skipping is great for co-ordination and stamina. Try to do as many different steps as possible.

- Run across the court, with your hands behind you. On alternate steps, flick one foot up to touch your hand.

Flexibility

- Jogging and arm swinging – forwards and backwards.

- Twisting your hips as you walk slowly forwards and backwards.

- Stretching and moving at the same time.

MENTAL TOUGHNESS

Tennis can be a difficult game mentally for the following reasons:

- You have to concentrate, but there is a lot of 'downtime' between points.
- You are on your own in singles.
- Often in junior tennis there are no umpires – you have to score for yourself and you might have to deal with an opponent who cheats.
- You might win the first set and be looking forward to winning the match – but a tennis match is played over three sets and you have to win two of them.

So there are many ways in which tennis is mentally more challenging than some other sports.

Keeping cool

There are a number of strategies that will help you keep your cool:

- Learn to forget about everything else when you get ready for the point. Concentrate on what you will do with the serve, or the return.
- Take no notice of other people when you are on the court – and be confident in yourself.

- Keep the score and say it out loud. Always play fair whatever the situation. Call your lines correctly. If opponents do not, politely ask if they are sure and then get on with the match. If the cheating continues, ask for an umpire.
- Never look back or ahead – the only thing that matters, and that you can do anything about, is the present point.
- Don't get down if you lose the first set – there are still two more you can win.
- Don't get excited if you win the first set – just be sure you win the first game of the next set and then a few more. You always need to win two sets!

Jennifer Capriati shows the determination that has won her many matches.

Junior tennis has a large variety of tournaments that you can enter. To play against different players, and really develop your game, you need to play matches. This will also help you to appreciate where you need to improve. You will need to get a rating to enter many tournaments. You can ask a coach to help you, or contact the Lawn Tennis Association Ratings department.

If you are a member of a club, you will find a number of tournaments for juniors, and many schools now take part in competitions.

Types of competition

There are knockout or championship tournaments, where you can only play while you are winning. Once you lose, you are out. But there are also a number of other types of tournament:

LADDER EVENT

This is a different sort of tournament and many schools have them. In this tournament every player is put on a rung of the ladder, and players can challenge each other to a match. Generally, you can only challenge a player one or two rungs above you. If you beat that player, you move up to their position on the ladder. The tournament is usually played over a few weeks, or even months, and the person on the top rung at the end of the time is the winner

ROUND ROBIN

In this type of tournament, players are put in groups of five or six players. Then, every player plays against every other player in their group (sometimes called boxes). Each time a player wins, two points are awarded. The winner of the group is the player with the most points after all the matches. Usually a round robin event is played over a day, but it might be just a morning or afternoon. The event does guarantee lots of matches.

LEAGUE MATCHES

These are events between a number of different teams of players, just like in netball or football. League matches are for either singles or doubles, or even both. There are usually four or six players in a team, and each singles player or doubles pair plays against their opposite number in the other team. At the end, all the matches are added up and one team will be the winner. The winning team earns league points, and the winner of the league is declared at the end of the season.

PLAYING DOUBLES

Apart from being great fun, playing doubles can be a great way of developing your game. You will become a better server and improve your volleying skills. You will learn all about angles, and learn how to change the direction of the ball you return, as well as working out where the spaces are on the court. If you get the chance, make sure you give it a go.

7 UNDERSTANDING THE RULES

Sometimes the rules of the game can seem quite complicated. You may have learnt them from other people, and sometimes they will not have told you quite correctly. There are some basic rules to follow.

- Nobody can make a decision on a ball being in or out until it has bounced. So if you are standing outside the court and you catch a ball before it bounces, you will lose the point. It does not matter that you knew it would have bounced out – it has not done so, and so no decision can be taken.
- If two things happen in a point, the first thing to happen will decide what happens next. For example, if the serve hits the net, but then the ball hits a player before it bounces, the let is the first thing so the serve is taken again.
- If players are on the wrong side of the court to serve or receive, and this is not noticed before the point is over, then the score stands – but the players go to the correct side for the next point.

One last point

At the beginning of a match, you and your opponent will toss the racket and one of you will make the first choice of these options: to serve first, to receive first, to choose the end of the court or to let the opponent choose.

You will notice that you can choose the end. If you make this choice, your opponent can choose to serve or receive.

So get to know the rules – it may matter at an important time, and could make the difference between winning or losing.

Now go out and enjoy your tennis. I'll see you at Wimbldeon one day!

For information on Ratings and Junior Competitions, contact the Lawn Tennis Association, Palliser Road, West Kensington, London W14 9EG. Telephone: 0207 381 7000. For details of a club near you, check the website: www.Lta.org.uk